Long on the Journey

Rev. M. Basil Pennington o. c. s. o.

Long on the Journey
The Reflections of a Pilgrim

Our Sunday Visitor Publishing Division
Our Sunday Visitor, Inc.
Huntington, Indiana 46750

ISBN: 0-87973-412-4
LCCCN: 88-63532

PRINTED IN THE UNITED STATES OF AMERICA

Cover design by Rebecca J. O'Brien

412

To
Aunt Marion
A WONDERFUL INSPIRATION FOR YOUNG AND OLD

Contents

A Word of Introduction 7

Good News 9

Keep Knocking 18

Eventide 26

'Father, Forgive Them' 34

Lessons of Life from a Death 45

Decapitating Conscience 52

A New Consciousness 61

Another Vocation 73

The Rosary 82

In His Steps 93

Hearing the Word of God 101

Tree Care 106

What About the Liturgy? 112

True Christian Greatness 119

Are We Laughing? 128

A Mother's Power 133

Be Like Our Mother 138

A Prayer for Those Growing Old 142

Beatitudes for Friends of the Aged 143

A Word of Introduction

I don't know at what age one can legitimately begin to say that she or he has been "long on the journey." Forty, fifty, sixty? Certainly at seventy, eighty, or ninety. Some days I feel I have been on the journey for a long, long, *long* time. It was at these times that some of these pages were first thought of and written down. I have tried to draw the inspiration and strength that I need from the traditional ways of prayer, from the Scriptures, from the teaching of the Church and the liturgy. These have helped me as I have journeyed on. God has been very good to me. Yet I have known some loneliness and have walked with it. I have known hurt and sorrow and loss. But underneath it all there has always been a joy. And this, above all, is what I want to share with you: my joy in the Lord and the joyful hope with which he has filled my journey.

I have shared only a few thoughts here. I have kept this book purposely short. If you find what I have written helpful, let me know, and I will write more for you.

Thank you for allowing me to share with you. Do pray for me. And I will pray for you.

Father Basil

Good News

When I think of the Annunciation, there is one thing that strikes me. Well, actually there are many things, but there is one facet that particularly touches me.

The moment of the Annunciation is undoubtedly — without exaggeration — the most significant moment in all human history. At this particular moment God in an almost unbelievable way stepped into our human history. Almost unbelievable — but most believable: the very source and foundation of our Christian faith. God became man. It is in itself enough. If he had done nothing more, it would have been enough to save our race and give us a claim to unending divine life. It was only because this Divine Lover was so eager to get us to understand how much he loves us that this moment of incarnation was in fact the first in the drama of the paschal mystery, leading to our Lord's passion and death and the hope-giving resurrection.

It was for Mary a stupendous moment. We don't even know exactly where it took place: in the privacy of her own room, in the garden, or at the village well, as one strong tradition insists. We don't know just how the archangel Gabriel communicated with her. Was it in human form — young or old, male or female? Or was it through a dream — as her husband would hear? (Probably not — she did have to respond.) Or was it an inner voice or a presence in her imagination? We don't know. But his presence was sure, his message clear. And it was good news.

It was certainly good news for the whole human race. We were in the bondage of sin. There was no way out but the promise made by a punishing God in the moment of inflicting exile. A savior would come. And now he was coming. As Saint Bernard so dramatically depicts it, all heaven and all creation waited in breathless expectation while Gabriel delivered his message, waiting to hear the Virgin's

response. It was good news for us all —
and Mary's response was part of the
good news. The benignity of our God:
human response is part of our salvation.

We have a Savior — good news,
indeed! For Mary it was much more
than that. She was to be the very
Mother of God. She still wonders at the
awesome fullness of her grace. Yet in the
absolute transcendence of her divine
maternity let us not lose sight of the
simple human reality. She was to be a
mother. She shared at this moment the
very common but most special joy that
millions of her sisters had had and
would have — a joy we men never quite
get in on — the joy of the moment when
a woman hears for the first time with
assuredness, "You are going to be a
mother." Undoubtedly, there was a
specialness in this case, not only because
of the nature of the Child but also
because of the nature of the conception
and its context. This woman had
committed herself to virginity. She did
not know man. She had courageously
given up forever the possibility of the joy
of motherhood. And now that joy was

wholly and unexpectedly given to her (and without any sacrifice to her virginity — her other great joy). What good news!

Like most good news in this vale of tears, it had its shadow. What would be Joseph's reaction? How would all this work out with her virginal husband? It was something to be concerned about. If Joseph agonized over it until the angel Gabriel came, we can be sure the woman who loved him — and was the source of his anguish — agonized also.

But we haven't come yet to the particular point that strikes me. There was this good news for Mary: she was to be a mother, the Mother of God. And there was more good news: "And behold, your kinswoman Elizabeth in her old age has also conceived a son; and this is the sixth month for her who was called barren" (Luke 1:36).

This is the thing that is most striking to me. ". . . Mary arose and went with haste into the hill country, to a city of Judah, and she entered the house of Zechariah and greeted Elizabeth" (Luke 1:39-40). Here, in the

moment of overwhelming good news —
wherein, she, Mary, was to be a mother,
the Mother of God — Mary so entered
into the good news about Elizabeth that
she seemingly forgot herself and rushed
to her cousin. Wouldn't it have been a
time to close the door on the world and
enjoy the wondrous presence? To devote
all her attention to the life within,
awaiting the first sensations of its
stirring? Or perhaps to worry about how
all this was going to work out with
Joseph? But Mary didn't think about
herself, about her own joy and concerns.
She thought of a cousin. And not a
particularly close one — an old woman
who lived far away and belonged to
another class of society. But a woman
who was, in spite of the goodness of it
all, going through all the difficulties and
uncertainties of a first pregnancy, made
more fearful by the burden of age. Mary
was there with her cousin as only a
relative who was sharing the same
mysterious experience could be.

One of the greatest plagues our
society suffers — and it is almost
universally experienced — is the soul-

numbing agony of loneliness. It accounts for so much of the promiscuous sex. Who wants to sleep alone? And for the alcoholism. Who can face the emptiness, the lack of understanding, the overwhelming negative self-image? It accounts for those who seek the dreamland of drugs, or the sensory distraction of endless television, or the nirvana of drugged sleep. How many know the imprisonment of loneliness and have the moral rectitude that restrains them from embracing one of these dehumanizing escapes? Yet they suffer the terrible suffering of being not just alone — that can be a blessing — but of being lonely. And that is a curse. Alas though, most of those who suffer loneliness in some way hug it to themselves. They cling to their loneliness. What is the payoff? Why do they hang on to it? It allows them to wallow in self-pity. It frees them, so they rationalize, from meeting the challenge of much of their potential to live and give life. Is it really worth it?

As I said, the particular point of the Annunciation story that strikes me is the way Mary, instead of clinging to her own personal good news and being all caught up with it, entered into the good news of Elizabeth and set out to share it as fully as she could — to be part of it. Instead of clinging to our own loneliness and being caught up in it, we can enter into the loneliness of our cousins — our sisters and brothers — in the Lord. We can reach out and enter into their loneliness and share it. This takes courage, but it is well worth it.

It took courage for Mary to set out across the alien land of the Samaritans to the strange hill country, into the midst of a people of another social level. You can be sure if you act courageously and reach out to another lonely person that the sound of your voice will cause a leap of joy within him or her.

Let's face it: we are afraid to reach out because we fear being repulsed. The initial surface reaction, the one we are allowed to see, may well be rejection to our outreach. The other may be too busy clinging to her or his loneliness. More likely, there is fear. Gratuitous love is, sad to say, seemingly such a rare commodity in our society that it is suspect. There is fear we might have ulterior motives, and then there is the fear of what might come after. What if we do for a time soothe the biting loneliness, but then we fade away? Won't the ensuing return of loneliness be all the worse for the memory of moments of love? We have to realize the possible presence of all these human reactions, and let them pass while we quietly continue to reach into the other's loneliness.

If we suffer from loneliness, there are other sufferers all about us. And "two lonelinesses who share" should equal "a communion that cures." There is not far from any of us a home for the retired and old. Don't content yourself with a sweeping general visit, spreading a smile to all, however good this may be. Take time to sit down with some*one* and make a real friend there. Let in a life to be shared with all its joys and sorrows. And if you can't get out, or are yourself a resident of such a home — there is a person in the next bed or the next room or down the hall. Or the attendant, who is a human with her or his own loneliness. And there is the phone and the pen. There is the outreach of prayer — loving concern that embraces other lives before and in God. It is oftentimes the interest even more than the response that is the cure of our own loneliness. But keep reaching. Where there is a will there is a way to enter into the loneliness of others and turn it into communion.

The particular point that struck me in the Annunciation story is this: when we realize that another human being is experiencing what we are experiencing and that we can set out and share it with that individual, that is good news — even when the thing we can share is in itself devastating. Old age, sickness, loneliness (the list seems endless) become, when shared, the stuff of human communion. And communion is the thing that makes us divine, because God is love. That is the good news!

Keep Knocking

Saint Luke tells us that "Herod the king laid violent hands on some who belonged to the Church. He killed James the brother of John with the sword; and when he saw that it pleased the Jews, he proceeded to arrest Peter also. This was during the days of the Unleavened Bread. When he had seized him, he put him in prison, and delivered him to four squads of soldiers to guard him, intending after the Passover to bring him out to the people" (Acts 12:1-4).

We can imagine how Peter was feeling at this time. James, who had been his companion, his fellow worker, his partner on the Sea of Galilee, and his partner in the adventures of life — together they had gone to seek and search, they had found John the Baptist, they had found Christ — had been cruelly beheaded. And now Peter was seized and there was no doubt about what the plans were in his regard. Have you ever thought how it would be to sit, hour after hour, contemplating the fact that you were soon to have your head cut off!

To add insult to injury, it was the great Feast of Passover and everyone outside — at least so it seemed to Peter looking out from the prison bars — was rejoicing as the feast was being celebrated. Life was at a high point, and here was Peter left alone in his cell with no one, it seemed, caring the least about his fate.

He was not quite alone. A couple of times already by miraculous intervention he had escaped from a prison cell. Herod was taking no chances. He had Peter chained, never free for a moment. But what are poor human guards to the angels of God? As Peter sat there his situation seemed desperate indeed. But. . .

Sometimes God lets us get pushed completely into a corner, into what seems to be an absolutely hopeless situation before he steps forward to help us. He does this so that we might more fully realize our need of his help, so that we might see that he is the source of salvation — that we can't do it ourselves.

In the case of Lazarus his sisters sent word to Jesus in good time that the brother whom they and he loved was sick. But Jesus tarried in coming. If he healed Lazarus before he died, people could say that Lazarus's own natural resources had brought him back to good health. If he raised Lazarus from the dead almost immediately after his death, as he did in the case of Jairus's daughter or even the son of the widow of Nain who was not yet laid in the grave, they could say the death was an illusion. The dead person was just in a deep coma and Jesus roused him. And so Jesus tarried and the situation became completely hopeless. "Martha, the sister of the dead man, said to him, 'Lord, by this time there will be an odor, for he has been dead four days' " (John 11:39). Only then did Jesus tell Lazarus to come forth from his burial place, and all saw the glory of God.

If the Lord had kept Peter from getting caught and imprisoned, Peter might have thought that he had eluded his persecutors by using his natural talents and abilities. Being in prison, reduced to a state of hopelessness, showed him and everyone else that liberation comes from the Lord.

Of course, the ultimate release and healing is that of eternal life. In our shortsightedness we don't always see that and think that the Lord has to come to our rescue here on earth. God has heaven and all eternity in which to respond to the deep aspirations of our prayer. Even when it seems he allows things to deteriorate to their very worst — witness, for instance, the fact that Peter ultimately was crucified — God is going to right it all and respond to all our deepest aspirations raised to him in confident prayer through ultimate victory in the kingdom of heaven. We should never give up on the Lord but always keep praying, keep knocking on his door: "Ask, and it will be given you; seek, and you will find; knock, and it will be opened to you" (Luke 11:9).

Luke goes on to tell us in the Acts of the Apostles: "The very night when

Herod was about to bring him out, Peter was sleeping between two soldiers, bound with two chains, and sentries before the door were guarding the prison; and behold, an angel of the Lord appeared, and a light shone in the cell; and he struck Peter on the side and woke him, saying, 'Get up quickly.' And the chains fell off his hands. And the angel said to him, 'Dress yourself and put on your sandals.' And he did so. And he said to him, 'Wrap your mantle around you and follow me.' And he went out and followed him; the angel was real, but [Peter] thought he was seeing a vision. When they had passed the first and the second guard, they came to the iron gate leading into the city. It opened to them of its own accord, and they went out and passed on through one street; and immediately the angel left him. And Peter came to himself, and said, 'Now I am sure that the Lord has sent his angel and rescued me from the hand of Herod and from all that the Jewish people were expecting' '' (12:6-11).

For the moment, Peter was free. He hastened to the home of friends. Perhaps this was the same house in which they celebrated the Last Supper and sought to hide after the crucifixion of Jesus, their leader. In any case Peter was not mistaken: ". . . many were gathered together and were praying" (Acts 12:12). We see a very agitated Peter, eager to get off the streets, eager to be embraced in the love of the community, pounding feverishly at the door. The prayer was going strong and it took time for someone to hear him; finally one did, and a servant girl was sent to see who was there. She recognized Peter's voice, but in her excitement, instead of opening the door and letting the poor man in, she ran in to tell everybody that it was Peter. So Peter was left standing outside pounding and pounding fruitlessly against the unyielding door while the people inside, who held him in such love, incredulously debated the meaning of the pounding.

Peter's experience here is not an uncommon one. So often when we cry out in our need, we cannot say exactly what we need. We may not even know ourselves. More often we just are not able to articulate it. We have to resort to some kind of pounding. And our cry — our pounding, so to speak — is not understood or believed. Perhaps we have always been the strong one and others can't quite hear that we do need help. Perhaps we are thought to be too far gone, too far out of it, to need to be included in the ordinary signs and expressions of community life and care. The great danger is that we will give up and stop pounding, stop sending messages.

With the lack of response we may well conclude that others just don't care. They don't want to be bothered with us any longer. It is too much of a burden to open their homes or their hearts to us. Peter might well have come to that conclusion — that these people didn't want a hunted man in their home. The fact was, the people inside were filled with love and concern for him. They just couldn't believe that the opportunity of expressing it was being given to them. They didn't understand the pounding at the door, even though it seemed perfectly obvious to Peter, and to us looking on. Unfortunately, the obvious is not always so obvious.

We need to keep knocking, to keep sending signals, because there is love and care in the depths of every human heart. And such love and care longs to express itself. But it is timid. Look in your own heart and see if that is not so. The human heart is a warm and loving place. But it is so, so vulnerable. It is just so afraid it will be rejected and hurt if it opens its door to let others in. So it needs clear signals that it is wanted.

We really do others a favor when we knock on their door and seek the shelter of their love, for most are lonely within, and longing for someone to come. But even if that is not the case, there is the caring and the longing to care. Let us take courage and keep knocking till we are heard and understood. We have been freed from our chains, oftentimes chains of pride and self-sufficiency, just so we can go knocking and give others the joy of caring for us. There are so many lonely people because so many have given up knocking.

Keep knocking!

Eventide

November has always been a difficult month for me. This was especially true when I was a young monk. In those days, before the incorporation of Thanksgiving and the Feast of Christ the King into the liturgical year, the liturgy spoke all about the end of the world. Everything was death and dying. The magnificence of a New England fall had given way to bare and barren trees not yet clothed in the winter mantle of Cistercian white. It was getting colder and colder in the monastery and we didn't put on the heat till the first Sunday of Advent — very liturgical and very economical! It was the eventide of the year and one felt it at every level of being.

Life has its eventide, too. And the month of November with its dedication to the holy souls, with its opening festivities and commemorations of the saints and the other departed souls, sends our thoughts in that direction. The eventide of life does tend to bring its dreary thoughts of the end of things as so many of life's activities wind down. The bright things of life are passing and the glow of eternal life is still a promise. Limbs grow cold and no amount of warmth seems to be able to warm them. Eventide.

A while ago I received a special grace, an unexpected one, and one that was well disguised. I was taken to visit a place called Eventide.

Eventide is the refuge for the destitute old folks of Kingston, Jamaica. As a young seminarian I had regularly visited the sick poor, especially older ones in the county hospital in Brooklyn, New York. It was a weekly journey that often cost much in the toll it took on my feelings, but it had many consoling joys, too. The worst I experienced in those Depression days in Brooklyn in no way prepared me for the tragedy of Eventide in Kingston.

The compound was large, surrounded by a very battered rusty old fence. The gates have long since disappeared. And, unfortunately, the inmates (I don't like the word, but it seems appropriate enough in this sad case) really miss the protection of those fences and gates. At night the destitute youth from the surrounding slums come out as marauders and strip the old and sick of whatever little they might possibly have and wreak havoc on the facilities of the institution, leaving it in a perpetual shambles. A few police watch during the day, but they are afraid to come out of the administration building at night. The wards in this home for the elderly and sick remind me of the barracks that housed the youthful trainees of the Civilian Conservation Corps back in the thirties or the army barracks that were hastily thrown up in the first days of World War II. The grounds all around them look as though they have gone through a war. A few trees have escaped, but little more. The blazing sun beats down on a parched and barren earth. Old folks sit about listlessly on the steps of the barracks or under the trees, in various degrees of undress and dishevelment. A few mangy mutts crawl about, too. How they survive in this place of so much human want is something of a mystery.

The sights inside the barracks are even more disheartening. Water is in scarce supply. The few nurses and dedicated lay helpers cannot begin to cope with the needs of so many. And many of the inmates are incapable of doing anything for themselves either because of mental deterioration or physical handicaps. To add to the overall pathos is the presence of a number of mentally retarded children who have been dumped in the midst of all this, for there is no other institution for them. The chaos, the stench, the filth, the ravages of malnutrition, the overall human misery is really too much to take. This is Eventide for the senior citizens of Jamaica, those who have no family to care for them. I have seen human misery in many places in the world — in the slums of New York, Haiti, Bombay, Manila, Calcutta, and post-civil-war Cadiz — but I have never seen it so concentrated and so naked, not even in the leprosariums of India, as it is in Eventide. Eventide is off limits for foreign visitors to Jamaica; even those, like ourselves, who are able to visit by special arrangements are not allowed to bring cameras. We can store the scenes only in our hearts. There is little chance of ever forgetting them.

Why did I call this visit a grace? Because I do not think I shall ever again experience my loneliness or my physical ills the same way I did before this visit. We all do experience a lot of loneliness in our lives, and it seems in some ways and at some levels to increase as the years go by. Our near ones and dear ones slip away. At the same time we are more aware of the joys and companionship that seem to fill the lives of the young ones around us. It is hard not to give way to some resentment that might overlay a certain envy or jealousy and which compounds the weight of our loneliness. But now, when I sense the waves of loneliness beginning to invade me, I go back to Eventide, to the bedside of one of those destitute and abandoned poor. How can I think of loneliness when I see such total abandonment? My feelings turn to compassion. I weep not for myself but for another. And a quiet sense of gratitude wells up for all that I have and all the care that does surround me. I may not have all that I want in the way of human intimacy, but I do have so much.

As to my physical ills, they seem so little now, and so pampered. There are the daily aches and pains. I may have lost much of my hair, and my teeth may be a bit loose; but, thank God, I do still have all my faculties. Eventide has helped me to put things in perspective. More important, it has helped me to grow in that most fundamental human attitude: compassion. When I am suffering for others and with others, even if they are far away, I am no longer alone. My life takes on some added meaning. And poor though I am, I search for little ways to help those so much poorer than I. We may not seem to be able to do much, but we can always reach out in love and prayer. That in itself will have effects that this world can never fully weigh.

If we begin to reach out, in the end

we will be the ones who most benefit. Our horizons will expand, bringing in a bit more of this world of ours into our lives, a bit more of its mystery, especially its paschal mystery where the passion of Christ is still somehow very present with its redemptive power and hope. As we reach out, our own lives will be filled with more life-giving love. Our own loneliness and concerns will fall into the background. I know. I speak from my own experience.

I feel I have expressed this all very ineptly. I found Eventide so overwhelming that I am sure I can never speak of it in any way that will be adequate. Some things just have to be experienced. Also, I don't feel I have really expressed well the other dimension that is behind my writing this. And that is my concern for you. I want you *not* to be drawn into your loneliness and pain, no matter how great it is, but to know the joy of going out to others, to know the empowerment of your love and concern. It certainly isn't necessary to go to Eventide in Jamaica to find sisters and brothers in great need. There are plenty of them in many American cities and towns. But it is necessary to be concrete. Maybe it is only when we meet the suffering Christ concretely in another human that we come to know the power of the redemption in ourselves, that we come to know by experience that the healing, redeeming love of Christ is truly in us.

As one of the great gifts of the liturgical renewal, the Church year now ends with the feast of Thanksgiving and a celebration of the ultimate triumph of Christ, our King. When gray days come upon us and thoughts of eventide press in, let us not turn in upon ourselves, but in thanksgiving for all that has been and will be, let us take something of the powerful healing love of Christ and reach out to another.

'Father, Forgive Them'

"Father, forgive them; for they know not what they do" (Luke 23:34). Really? ". . . they do not know what they do?"

Those brawny Roman soldiers knew well enough what they were doing as they mercilessly pounded those spikes into the quivering flesh of their victim. True, there may have been some pity lurking in their hearts, some sense of shame. But this "King of the Jews" was not a Roman, not a citizen, therefore hardly a man. Perhaps what was behind their mockery in the barracks before the forced march to Calvary was an effort to make their victim something less than a fellow human being. Besides, they were only soldiers doing their duty.

But since the Nuremberg trials for war criminals and the shameful events at My Lai we more commonly realize that "soldiers doing their duty" are still men like the rest of us with personal responsibility and the obligation to form their own consciences and act accordingly. Duty though it be, these men were inflicting a terrible suffering upon a fellow human. They knew what they were doing. And yet, of course, they did not. They did not know that this man was not just a fellow human. He was the very Son of God — God himself. And he was totally innocent of any crime his enemies might have alleged or any other. He was the very incarnation of goodness, justice, and love. In many ways the soldiers did *not* know what they were doing. Their victim himself had declared: ". . . he who delivered me to you has the greater sin" (John 19:11).

Those men of the Sanhedrin — they surely knew what they were doing. It was something they had long wanted to do. They waited for the opportunity. When it came, they very deliberately used it. They paid off the traitor and carefully planned the final capture. They lined up false witnesses. They departed from many of the procedures of normal justice in their eagerness to get the thing accomplished and over with.

They screamed and schemed for his blood before the procurator of the hated Gentiles. They knew what they were doing.

And they didn't. They so cloaked what they were doing in righteousness, so rationalized, that they even convinced themselves (at least for the most part — conscience is not easily turned off) that what they were doing was good: ". . . it was expedient that one man should die for the people" (John 18:14). They knew this man was special; he had power from God; he was, in sum, a godly man. But that he was more than man? That he was the very God they worshiped in the Temple? For these staunch monotheists, such an affirmation was absolutely incredible — without the gift, the insight, of faith. They hadn't received that gift. How responsible were they for that?

They did not know, really, what they were doing. As guilty as they might have been, rationalization, darkness of mind, passion, fear, and a host of other surging emotions prevented them from seeing what they were really doing. We never choose evil as evil. We always choose it under some guise of good. Sometimes we are very aware that we are choosing our own good over the good of another, or a partial, lesser good over a greater good. That is pretty much the extent of our evil.

Jesus, who lived and died for others, even in his moments of greatest agony and human pain and degradation, thought of others. As he hung there, he was aware of all the forces of darkness that had clouded the understanding of his murderers. And his compassion, which is above all his attributes, spoke out: "Father, forgive them; for they know not what they do." He was right, of course. Up to a point, no matter how evil and guilty they were, they did not know what they were doing. Jesus in his compassion considered this.

Jesus always did the things that pleased the Father. He was one with the Father and acted in all things as his Father. Perhaps he was recalling that day long ago when an angry and discouraged prophet was wallowing in depressing self-pity because the Father had shown mercy to a sinful but repentant city. As Jonah complained, the Father replied: ". . . should I not pity . . . a hundred and twenty thousand persons who do not know their right hand from their left. . . ?" (Jonah 4:11). Jesus did not miss the malice and evil present. He felt it not only in his body so brutally abused and soon to be totally destroyed but also to the very depth of his sensitive soul. Yet he chose to look at the blinding ignorance, the human weakness, all that would excuse his executioners, and to reach out to them in compassion. Obviously, as he asked the Father to forgive them, he totally forgave them from his heart.

Forgiveness is at the very heart of Christianity, of being a disciple of Jesus. He had told us: ". . . learn from me; for I am gentle and lowly in heart, . . ." (Matthew 11:29). Here he exercised meekness and humility — not virtues easy to come by, especially for "red-blooded" Americans. In this ultimate moment of his life, of his teaching and his life's witness, he first of all taught us forgiveness.

Perhaps nothing so plagues human life and wrings it of its joy and fulfillment as does unforgiveness. As we grow older, the fund of unforgiveness can become an immense burden. The unwillingness to forgive can totally destroy a relationship, leaving a terrible vacuum in our lives. If we let unforgiveness deprive us of too many of our relationships we pave the way for a great loneliness.

But even where the lack of forgiveness does not destroy relationships, it can yet rob them of much of their power to nurture and bless our lives. No relationship can be full, open, and Christian as long as one of the partners refuses to forgive from his or her heart. No matter how much we might do with the other person and enjoy that person and being with him or her, if we are harboring any least bit of unforgiveness, the relationship will at depth be bitter. This is often the reason why enduring marriages are not the fullness of joy that they can and ought to be. One or both of the partners are holding on to some grievance, little or great, even as they move through life together, even enjoying many things together.

Where we get caught is that we put conditions on our forgiveness. We say we will forgive if the offender apologizes, or at least admits his or her fault, or at the very least stops offending. That was not the case with our Master on Calvary. And if we would be his true disciples and pursue his way to complete happiness and freedom, we must follow his example. Even if the offensive person does not see how he or she is offending or refuses to admit responsibility or to change a way of acting, we as disciples of Jesus, if we want to be true disciples, and indeed if we want to find happiness and fullness in life — which is love — we must forgive. We cannot make our forgiveness conditional, nor dependent on what others do. In the end, we are the only victims of our own unforgiveness and the agents of our own forgiveness.

This does sound like folly, doesn't it? To forgive someone for offending us, violating us, even while that person continues to do so. But isn't that precisely what Jesus is doing, all the time, with us and everyone else? Isn't that precisely what the saints have done — Saint Stephen, the first martyr, who prayed for Paul and his other murderers, right down to Saint Maximilian Kolbe, who starved to death in a Nazi death camp? This is indeed a part of the folly of the cross that we followers of Jesus Christ embrace as the way to have life and have it more abundantly.

This is not easy. In fact, it is totally beyond our reason and our strength. We can do it only in the wisdom of Christ and with the help of his grace.

I live in a large community, a real family. I am embraced with a lot of love, care, and compassion. But I also "suffer" constantly from a certain amount of jealousy, insensitiveness, resentment. There are fellow monks who want to make me over into their image of what the ideal monk should be, and will not accept me being the monk that I am. There are those who resent my gifts — and the way I use them — and those who resent my lack of gifts (my singing is probably winning more than one monk a higher place in heaven!). And I have to live with the pain and humiliation of knowing that I do fail my brothers and cause them suffering in many ways, offend them in many ways. I need their forgiveness and I need to constantly forgive myself. And I need to forgive all my brothers, even while they continue to make me "suffer," or else my life would be constantly plagued and truncated by the hardness of unforgiveness. I could not be nurtured by the love and compassion that is truly there. And I could not say that I am honestly trying to be a true disciple of Jesus Christ.

The same situation arises at times in every human relationship or network of relationships, at home or at one's place of work or in any other gathering of friends and associates. It arises above all in marriage, which in our Christian dispensation is the sacrament of Christ's love for his Church — that love which expressed itself on the cross in compassionate forgiveness and continues even as we continue to offend such goodness and love. A married couple who live forgiving and compassionate love even as they daily fail each other — because they are sinful human persons as are we all — are the true sacrament of Christ's love for us all. They are making space in their marriage for the greatest possible love and happiness.

The reality that drew pagans to the early Christian communities was expressed by one of them: "See how these Christians love one another!" They had learned from their Master on the cross, who forgave even as he suffered.

If we constantly practice this Christlike forgiveness through all our lives, toward our spouse, our children, our family, our friends, our associates, the relationships of our lives will not only perdure, but mature and ripen to bless our later years. However, if we terminate or limit relationships by unforgiveness there may well come a time when there will be not even one full and open relationship to grace our lonely lives.

Forgiveness is a wonderful thing. It

is never too late. Today, at this moment, we can forgive from our hearts each and every offense we have ever suffered or are suffering. We can at this moment open all the channels for a new free flowing of love. We can, in the power of Christ's compassion, not only understand that "they do not know what they do" — even as we don't: whoever sees with constancy the tremendous beauty and goodness of each daughter and son of God, made in his own image? — but truly make his prayer our own: "Father, forgive them; for they know not what they do." And even as we pray the prayer, we will know that our own hearts have expanded, and new floods of wonderful, compassionate love are flowing through.

We are sons and daughters of the Cross, and its lessons are the Way, the Truth, and the Life.

Lessons of Life from a Death

On the second day of Christmas we celebrate the first martyr. Well, not exactly. Two days later we realize there were others. *Non loquendo sed moriendo confessi sunt*: "Not by speaking but by dying they proclaimed" the newborn King, these Holy Innocents. Yet in the first day after Christmas we do revel in the manifest witness of the holy deacon and first martyr, Stephen: "Behold, I see the heavens opened, and the Son of Man standing at the right hand of God" (Acts 7:56). The mission that began in the humble stable has run its course. He has looked on his Lowly One, he has exalted the Humble. Born rejected — there was no room for him among men and women in the inns of this world — even as he is exalted by God he is still rejected by men.

In our last chapter we spoke of

Saint Stephen. In his condemnation we have a most blatant example of prejudice. His judges literally clamped their hands over their ears and shouted at the top of their voices so as not to hear the witness of the truth. What need have we of further witness? These are indeed men of malevolent intent. Or are they?

When in dialogue, in our own search for truth, whether it be a dialogue with an individual person or with history, we need to step around to the other side and see how things look from there. Or as our early American brothers would say: "Don't judge another until you have walked in his moccasins."

Look at it from the perspective of the Jewish Sanhedrin. The Jewish people, God's Chosen People, were but a little congregation among the vast nations that surrounded them on every side. They had received a very precious revelation: "Know, Israel, your God is one God. There is no other God like him." They preserved with difficulty — hadn't even some of their own greatest kings like David fallen away? — this sacred heritage of monotheism. And now, this young man was daring to proclaim that Jesus, that condemned and crucified blasphemer, was standing at the very right hand of God in his glory. Such a blasphemy could not be tolerated. Pious ears could not be allowed to be tainted by it. The only adequate response was outrage.

We know, of course, that if these men rested quietly in the truth they possessed and in that peaceful assurance listened to all that Stephen had to say they could have discerned that he in no way contradicted their most sacred heritage. Rather, he proclaimed its fulfillment — just as the hopeful lights of Hanukkah find their fulfillment in the true Light who is our Christ. But these men, leaders and teachers though they be, did not possess the truth deeply enough and purely enough to be able to hear anything that they perceived threatened it or the position of superiority they might derive from the possession of it.

Let us put ourselves in their moccasins, or rather their sandals, for a minute. Suppose grandson Stephen or

the new young deacon in the parish
begins to extol the qualities of Buddha
at the monthly meeting of the Holy
Name Society or the Rosary Sodality.
What would be our spontaneous
reaction? But didn't the most solemn
source of authoritative teaching in our
Church, an ecumenical council,
speaking in the power of the Holy Spirit,
tell us that we are not only to respect
and reverence but even to foster all that
is good and true in the great religions of
the world? If we possess our fullness of
truth peacefully in our hearts and let fall
away all the prejudices and
misconceptions that may have hedged it
around when we were less secure, we
might be able to hear that Buddha was
indeed a great saint. And we might learn
something from the holiness of his life:
the importance of interiority and
freedom from possessions and prestige.

But my purpose here is not to
defend Buddha or any of the other
uncanonized saints of times past and
present. It is rather to help us get hold of
one of the important lessons we can
draw from the heroic witness and

martyrdom of Saint Stephen, and to apply it to our own lives: the need to remain open even when we know we have the truth. For, in fact, we do not possess the truth, and we do not want to. We want the Truth to possess us. The Truth is something — or rather Someone — infinitely bigger than us, for he said: "I am the Truth." The Truth is God, and he has multiple ways of manifesting himself, to lead us day by day into all truth. One of the things that makes life unendingly interesting, though we walk through eighty or a hundred summers, is this reality. God ever has more of his truth, his goodness, and his beauty to reveal to us — if we but remain open and let him speak to us by whatsoever messenger he will.

One of the things that threaten to entice us to close down is the desire for security. If we can get our Catholic faith gathered into a nice neat bundle we can feel we have a secure hold on it and need not fear. But the reality of God is even bigger than the dogmas of our faith: " 'What no eye has seen, nor ear heard, nor the heart of man conceived, what

God has prepared for those who love him,' God has revealed to us through the Holy Spirit" (1 Corinthians 2:9-10). Our security is in love — not in knowledge. The Spirit of Love will give us all the knowledge we need as we need it. Jesus promised at the Last Supper that he would send him to teach us all things, and recall to our minds all that he had taught us.

The Sanhedrin's minds were closed to Stephen because he threatened their position as the secure depositories of *the* truth and the position of preeminence this gave them. Sometimes we are closed to the good qualities and insights of other churches and religions because we want to pride ourselves on having the religion that has the corner on all truth. In Christ we do have all truth, but we don't understand it fully. Others' insights can help us to possess and benefit by what we already have.

There is another lesson I would like to draw briefly from Saint Stephen's martyrdom, and that is the power of prayer. As he fell to his knees under the force of the battering stones that were to pound out his life he prayed. He commended himself to Jesus and he prayed for those who were killing him. Among them was Saul of Tarsus, fully in accord with the executioners. Hardly could either Stephen or Saul have imagined that the next time the heavens would open to reveal the Son of Man it would be for this persecutor for whom the martyr now prayed. And that the prayer of the dying martyr would give birth to the greatest witness to the exaltation of the Son of Man. Prayer is answered, perhaps years later, in ways beyond all our expectations.

In the end, even if we have to suffer persecution and martyrdom, if we are men and women of faith and forgiving love, as was Stephen — we shall all together, even with our persecutors, see the Son of Man in his glory and share in that glory. But even on the journey there we can be daily enlightened by his Presence if we will quietly hold the truths of his Love and remain with ears and eyes and hearts wide open to every manifestation of his Truth and his Love.

Decapitating Conscience

We all know the story of Saint John the Baptizer and his fate. The mission to be a social conscience is not a happy one. We have seen that so much in our own times. We think of the archbishop of San Salvador who, as he was offering the holy sacrifice of the Mass, suddenly entered most fully into the sacrifice of the Great Martyr. We think of Franz Jaegerstatter and Saint Maximilian Kolbe. And we think of those who perhaps paid a lesser price, but still one of incalculable cost: Dorothy Day, whose life was ever on the line for the poor. I see again this very old and worn woman, venerated by millions, being roughly dragged off to jail. I know something of the rejection and alienation Thomas Merton experienced when he spoke out. All true followers of Jesus who himself was a social conscience and was crucified for it.

Jesus' beloved cousin, called to be

so much a part of his Cousin's mission, had to be faithful to his difficult call. In that fidelity he courageously, publicly, rebuked the powerful King Herod when he told him it was not right for him to live with his brother's wife. Herod and his pseudo-wife, Herodias, responded differently to this "conscience."

Herodias conceived a murderous hatred and wanted to kill John. This is the way many respond to conscience. They want to silence it at all costs. They turn to drink and seek to envelop conscience in an alcoholic haze, where it is heard, if at all, only as some blurred message. Or they turn to drugs and go off into outer space with its fanciful albeit at times discordant harmonies. The voice of conscience cannot reach these foreign spaces. Or they sit every spare moment, when the voice of conscience might break through, before the "boob-tube," letting its idle and distracting chatter drown out any message from conscience. TV's violence and lust dwarf and justify one's own "little peccadillos."

To kill, to mute conscience, how

much of life's precious time and potential is dissipated on this fruitless quest! We can kill conscience by killing humanity. Liquor and drugs and mindlessness, of course, can lead to that, to insanity in a lesser or greater degree or to a total dehumanization. But most who attempt to kill conscience are not so relentless and successful as Herodias — successful at least in regards to killing the "Conscience," John the Baptist; in fact, her own conscience tore at her until her miserable death. Efforts to kill conscience produce for most only passing results, some hours of false escape, only to have conscience come back with one more accusation to make, one more betrayal of self, of life and love and God.

Herod responded to John, to conscience, in another way. He tried in a way to tame him, locking him up. He feared him, he restricted him, he was attracted by his evident goodness, a goodness that spoke to Herod of the hidden potential of his own life. John the Conscience was a disturbing influence in Herod's life and in his relationships, especially in his sinful relationship with Herodias. Yet he did not want to eliminate him, for within the rebuke lay a hope for this weak man. He failed in many ways. He sinned grievously. If he killed conscience he might enjoy his sin more, but then he would have no hope beyond his sin. And he knew only too well that his sinful life was not adding up to happiness. There had to be ultimately something more, or life wasn't worth living.

And so he kept "Conscience," but imprisoned, so he could listen to him when he wanted to and ignore him when he wanted to. Until the great betrayal. The source of this betrayal is the source that leads many of us to decapitate, at least for the moment, our own consciences; and that source is human respect, summed up (in Herod's case) in these words: ". . . because of his oaths and his guests, he commanded it to be given [it being whatever Herodias's daughter wanted]" (Matthew 14:9). He had foolishly gotten himself into an awkward position — how often when we have drunk too much do we put ourselves in foolish positions? How often does our bragging get us into trouble? — and he was so trapped by a false ego that depended on what others thought that he let his own "conscience" be killed.

Human respect is a powerful force. We see it so tragically in the lives of our young people. No matter how lovingly parents work at instilling true values into the lives of their children, they have to stand by, oftentimes feeling completely helpless, as the peer pressure takes over. They can only pray that the pressures their children encounter will not be too destructive and that that fragile developing personality will emerge and refind its true freedom in self-knowledge.

Human respect can enslave us because we do not know our true selves and we identify ourselves by what others think of us. This is the way we necessarily start out in life. But it is something we should outgrow through knowledge of our true self, that uniquely beautiful image and participation of the divine beauty that each one of us is. If we identify ourselves with a false self created by what others think of us, then when we are confronted with a situation where we must choose between what others think and conscience, this appears to us as a choice between continuing to exist and conscience, and conscience is easily the loser.

Practically, though, how can we come to know our true self and be free from an enslaving human respect? Human respect is so powerful because it is so close to the source of true self-knowledge and freedom. The only way we come to truly know ourselves is to see ourselves reflected back to us in the eyes of someone who loves us. When someone truly loves us for our very selves, the image that person reflects back to us is our true self. When someone "loves" us for some aspect of our lives, good or bad, true or false, this is what he or she reflects back to us as our being, at least in that individual's eyes. We are fortunate indeed if we have in our lives one or more who love us for our very selves.

Because we are by creation the very

image of God and by re-creation in baptism partakers of the divine childship of Jesus, the only Lover who can fully reflect back to us the fullness of our true self with all its beauty, power, and goodness is God himself. And he is a Lover who is always available. This is why quiet prayer and meditation are so important in our lives. It is only when we quiet down and sit with the Lord, letting everything else go for the moment (he can take care of the world without us for a few minutes, don't you think?), that we can open ourselves to the experience of his totally affirming love, the affirmation of our own priceless beauty and goodness. We will know that at every moment God brings us forth in his love. If others do not appreciate us, well . . . they are just missing the boat. God does! He appreciates us as no one else does — even though he knows our sinfulness through and through. That's why he became our Savior and took care of all of that.

There are many ways in which we can meditate. One very simple and effective way from our early Christian tradition is Centering Prayer. It is very simple — though not always easy. We sit comfortably, close our eyes, and turn to God dwelling in the center of our being — he promised to dwell there. We give ourselves to him in love, saying: "Lord, I know you are here. I love you, and for these twenty minutes I want just to be with you." Then, to keep present to him, we take up our favorite name for him — Jesus, Lord, Father, Love, whatever name we most frequently use when talking to him — and gently, interiorly, repeat it as we need to remain present to him in love. Whenever we become aware we are thinking of something else, or listening to something else but him, with our prayer name we gently return to him. At the end of our meditation time we might like to pray slowly the prayer Jesus taught us: Our Father. . . . (For those readers who might be interested in books I have written on Centering Prayer, here are three that are available in the Doubleday Image paperback series: *Centering Prayer, Daily We Touch Him*, and *A Place Apart.*)

Once we know our true selves, human respect can no longer lead us to decapitate our conscience, to betray it only to have it rise up again to accuse us of yet another betrayal of ourselves and of our God. In the knowledge of our own beauty and goodness, seen daily in the eyes of God in meditation, we can fully enter into freedom to be our true selves and rejoice in the wonder of our being, happy to have conscience guide us along the way to unending, blissful life.

A New Consciousness

We want to leave behind our self-centeredness and grow in an effective consciousness that God is the Center, our Center, the Center of all that is. We want to come to know Reality and live lives that are shaped by Reality and not by illusion, fabrication, and self-deceit.

This is what we mean by "transformation of consciousness." "Transformation" — a big word, but one that is easy to break down. "Tion" implies a certain permanence in the state described. "Trans" implies a going over, a change of position: "transport" — to carry over; "transfer" — to take one's self to a different place; "transition" — coming into a different situation. So, "transformation" means changing the "form" of our consciousness, coming into a new state of consciousness. "Consciousness" is the way we perceive things, the context within which we hold them.

With a transformation of consciousness we come to see things differently. The change we want, of course, is to come to see things as they really are — to see them as God sees them.

In scriptural language, this is rebirth in Christ: ". . . unless one is born anew, he cannot see the kingdom of God" (John 3:3). This has happened to us, essentially, in baptism. We were buried with Christ in the waters. We died to ourselves — our false selves, the person of sin, and rose again, as we came in out of the waters to a new life in Christ. I am happy that baptism by immersion is being restored to practice in the Catholic Church. It has always been used in some other Christian Churches. It so much more fully brings out the meaning of the rite.

At baptism we are brought to a new level of being. (Let me note that when I say "baptism," I usually mean to include baptism of desire — the desire to do what is right as one perceives it — the means whereby the majority of the human family come into the order of grace.) We are made partakers of the divine life and nature. If we are to be integral, what has happened at the level of being has to be appropriated also at the level of consciousness. As divinized men and women, we need a Godlike consciousness; we need to see things as God sees them, if we are to act in accord with our renewed nature.

At our natural birth, our perception makes us the center of the universe, of all that is. We are a little bundle of potential, much in need, very conscious of our needs. That is our first consciousness: the things we need. (Soon enough we begin to confuse what we need and what we want.)

As our consciousness begins to expand, we become aware of those persons who supply our needs: mother, father, family, and so on. The circle expands with the years.

In time, largely under the tutelage of these significant persons, we come to see what we do as being significant. "Mama won't love Johnny if he doesn't eat his spinach." (Why do we always pick on spinach — a perfectly good vegetable?) "Melanie is Daddy's good little girl, if she puts away all of her dolls."

There is something very sad in this. A parent's love, if it is true to its nature, is wholly gratuitous. No matter what a child does, no matter how he or she acts, good parents will still love their child. In this they are a sacrament of God's love — that wholly gratuitous love that brought us from nonbeing into being and sustains us at every moment. When parents begin to say things like "Mama won't love Johnny if he doesn't eat his spinach," and all the other forms this can take, they are trading on their parental love. This love is the most precious thing a child has. It is being bartered for small gains. The effect of this — which can and often does last a lifetime — is devastating. The message the child begins to receive is that he or she has to earn love. The other side of this is the message that we are not lovable in ourselves. It opens the door to all kinds of acting out to try to win the love that we feel fundamentally we do not deserve.

Because the parents are the first sacrament of God's love in a child's life, this attitude passes over into our understanding of that love. We begin to think that we must in some way earn God's love. Yet we can never be, of ourselves, worthy of it. The effect here cannot be worse, for such an understanding of divine love is a total profanation of it. Nothing can win God's love, for he is the source of all love and all that is to be loved. God's love is absolutely gratuitous. It is so great it makes what it loves worthy of the love it receives. The effect of a false understanding of God's love is paralyzing. We know we can fool some people at least some of the time. We can hide from them that unlovableness of which we are convinced and by external performance — provided we don't let them get too close — we can win some kind of love, or at least some respect and friendship that will soothe the loneliness of our lives. But there is no fooling God. He knows us through and through. He knows fully our unlovableness. How can we win his love? The answer to this false question has led to all sorts of aberrations. Many have not tried to answer it. They have just shut God out of their lives as someone they can't deal with.

I would certainly urge parents, especially parents of younger children, never to trade off the infinitely precious commodity of their parental love for some temporary gains. It is not worth it. The cost in the end can be astronomical. It can cost everything. Every child needs all the security and love he or she can possibly get.

But to get back to our evolution of consciousness — although all we have just said is certainly not aside from this consideration — as we grow we tend, largely because of the way others mirror us back to ourselves, to identify ourselves with what we have, what others think of us, and what we can do. We tend to construct a false self made up of those elements: what we have, what we do, what others think of us. This becomes the way we think of ourselves and present ourselves to others.

Reflect just a moment. How often when a man introduces himself does he not immediately add what he does — or gives you his business card. "I am Joe Jones. I work at Sperry's." "I am Phil Donovan. I am a professor over at C.U." Women do not tend to do this so much. Perhaps it is because, up until recently, what most of them are doing — homemaking — was not held in particular regard; it was not perceived as adding anything to their identity. But they perhaps made up for this lack of doing by the display of what they had. It is only now that men seem to be catching up with women in wearing their gold and silver and gems. The right car, the right address, the right club are seen as significant. And what about name droppers?

We can immediately see the consequences of such a false self-identification. When we create such a false self, we have created a very, very fragile self. The true self, the inner person, is experienced not at all, or only as something hollow. We depend wholly on what is without for our meaning and existence, and it can so easily be lost. Thomas Merton wrote of this in *The New Man*, his finest and deepest theological work: "Why must we live in the shadow-kingdom of beings who can never quite believe that they themselves exist? Without the living God (without a center) men become little helpless gods, imprisoned within the four walls of their own weakness and fear. They are so conscious of their weakness that they think they can only subsist by snatching from others the little that they have, a little love, a little knowledge, a little power."

Recently I saw a grown man almost cry when he lost a glove. It wasn't that the glove was particularly special, it was just that he had so identified himself with what he had that it was a part of himself that was lost. We can find ourselves seriously betraying ourselves to please others, because the false self lives in their estimation of us. This is one of the reasons why loneliness is so devastating. In the moment we perceive no one is thinking of us and caring for us we seem to cease to exist. When we can no longer do the things we have been doing, we are demolished. Isn't this the sad story of many men at retirement? For forty years or more they have said, "I am Joe, who works at Sperry's." "I am Phil, who teaches at C.U." What are they going to say now? An identity is lost — and all too frequently a life.

Because such a construct — this false self made up of what I have, what I do, and what others think — is so fragile, it leads to a great deal of defensiveness. We have to protect who we are. An open generosity is much too risky, unless it is essential to keep people thinking well of us. Because what we have, and what we can accomplish, and what others think of us can be limited by what others do, a real competitiveness comes into our lives. We cannot rejoice over others' good fortune — it might result in their getting some of the acclaim we would get, or their getting ahead to our detriment. We tend to try to get ahead, stepping on other people's heads.

God shows up in this also. He is the person out there whom we most have to get to think well of us by our doing the right things so that we will get the real goodies, the ones that last forever. We have reduced God to our level of acting — a real idol, not the true God.

One of the effects of all this is a deep resentment. To get what I want I have to do what all these others want, what God wants. I can't do what I want and get what I want. So we resent people, and even God. We probably are not too conscious of this — after all, we are trying to please these people so that they will think well of us. We can't let our resentment out. In fact, we dare not even let ourselves be in touch with it, for it would make our task of pleasing these people too difficult. We have to hold that we like these people, even as they truncate our freedom to be. Such suppressed resentment is dangerous. I believe it is at the root of much of the anger and hostility so frequently erupting in our society. When we cannot act against those whom we really resent, the suppressed resentment — unless we find some way to dissipate it — will eventually erupt chaotically and without direction. Even the most innocent become its victims.

What then are we to do? We need to realize — and even to know by experience — that God is not out there somewhere as the Great Rewarder or Punisher. I can remember from my earliest days a stained-glass window. It depicted a triangle with a great seeing eye in the middle of it. God was keeping an eye on me. Our God is out there — he is everywhere. And he does see everything — with his eye of love. But where is his favorite dwelling place on earth, in all creation? Where does he most immediately and significantly touch us and our lives? It is within us that the Father and the Son and the Holy Spirit have chosen to make their dwelling.

The shift of consciousness, the transformation of consciousness that we want, is to come to realize and to know by experience, that God does dwell within us, with all his creative love, ever bringing us forth in his love and goodness. There is nothing we did, can do, or ever will do to earn this constant presence of affirming, caring, creating love.

When we come to realize that God himself is ever with us, affirming our beauty, goodness, and significance by constantly sharing with us something of his own divine being and beauty, how can we care what others think — those who know us so much less? If you don't appreciate me, you are missing the boat. God appreciates me!

With this transformation of consciousness, which puts God experientially at the center, we are born to a new freedom. Or rather, we take possession of that freedom that was given to us in our rebirth in Christ, the freedom of the well-loved children of God.

Another Vocation

I don't know if there is anyone around who would remember "those good old days" when the family gathered sometime in January to make the year's supply of candles so that come Candlemas they would be able to bring them to the church for blessing. When I was on Mount Athos in northern Greece a few years ago I had the joy of taking part in this ancient "rite." For several days we made preparations, bringing in the necessary firewood and the blocks of wax that had been made when the honey was separated in the fall, getting the equipment out of the attic, planning the shifts of the monks who would keep the project going around the clock until it was done. It was a big project there, where there is no electricity and candles are still the main means of light; plus the fact that "the bigger the feast, the more the candles" — many candles were needed for the liturgical celebrations.

It went on, night and day, for three days — the candle-making. The wax was melted in a large cauldron over an open fire, then the molten wax was poured into a cylinder about three feet high. First, the string that would make the wicks was dipped (doubled over so that there would be a loop at the top) and then rolled. Next, five wicks were hung on a crown so that they could all be dipped into the cylinder at the same time. They were dipped three times and then allowed to cool while other crowns were dipped, then dipped again. And so on, until each of the candles reached the desired diameter. We watched them grow, bit by bit, and then stacked them and watched the pile grow bit by bit, until, at last, a year's supply was accumulated. It was quite fascinating.

So it was on every farm and homestead in the old days, when each household that could, would make its own candles. And if they were rich in wax, they would make some for sale, too, for the townsfolk. Come the second of February someone from each family would be going to the church, bringing the coming year's supply of candles to be blessed so that they might bring a blessed light to their homes.

Today, candles are special things, particularly fitting for times of celebration or moments of religious significance. They have not lost their rich symbolism. The wax represents Christ's flesh, the wick his soul, and the blessed light the flame of his divinity. We may not be expected to bring our candles to church now, but it is important that we do bring blessed candles home, and have this presence in our homes. They will be there for moments of heightened religious significance, especially when the Eucharistic Lord comes into our home. In times of sickness, storms, or any distress, we can light our blessed candles and be comforted by the warmth of their light, assured of the presence of the Lord with the warmth of his love and care. At our times of prayer we might want to light them to proclaim his presence and center our presence to him. The blessed candle is a good use of the sacramental.

February second was chosen as

Candlemas, the day to bring candles to church, because it is the Feast of the Presentation, the day another family — Mary and Joseph — brought the Light of the World to the Temple. This feast completes, as it were, the Christmas cycle. God's great gift, his very Son, is returned to him. It is fully and publicly acknowledged that this firstborn is *the* Firstborn. Like every firstborn, but in ways that infinitely transcend that of any other, this Firstborn belongs to God, his Father. Yet, like every other, the Father allows him to be purchased by a people as their very own. No, it wasn't so much a turtledove that "ransomed" him, but a Mother's love. God is ours for the price of love — no other. And Mary is ready to teach us how to love so that we are worthy to have the Son of God as our own.

On that day when the Mother of Love brought this most precious Candle, the Light of his People Israel, into the Temple, there were two there to welcome him. At Bethlehem angels came and so did the poor shepherds and their little lambs. At Epiphany the Wise

Men, the powerful kings, came; they
were the rich, the great of this world
with their rich and meaningful gifts.
Now it was the elderly, the diminishing,
the senior citizens' turn. Two came
forth, a man and a woman, for all belong
equally to God, are equal in his sight.
We can learn from this elderly pair.

One of them was continuing in his
life's profession, still doing his work. If
we are still laboring, let us be sure it is
for the same motive that inspired this
holy man, and not because we are
clutching to this world and afraid to let
go. Simeon was beautifully detached.
He was ready to go: Now you can
dismiss your servant, O Lord. He
remained at his task only to serve. He
had only one purpose: to celebrate and
confirm the presence of Christ in his
world as the sign and source of salvation.
He knew the goodness of our God and he
waited with joyful expectation, knowing
that all his true expectations would be
fulfilled, and more than fulfilled.
Whatever our profession, our work, if we
are true Christians this is what we are
about.

Anna, the other of our two models, represents those who have chosen to retire. Look how she has used her retirement: in prayer, in fasting, in the Temple. If we are blessed with more leisure in the reclining years it is so that we can enter into and develop more fully the contemplative dimension of our lives and hasten the coming of Christ into our world. It is so that, like Anna, when he comes to us we can receive him with peace and joy. We have time now to read the Scriptures, to say our beads, to go frequently, if not daily, to Mass and Communion, or just to sit, enjoying his presence, perhaps burning our blessed candle or just being aware of the sanctuary lamp of our own love burning in our hearts. There is time for all that now. Let us use the time well.

Some senior-citizen homes, communities, and programs try to fill their participants' lives with distractions: all sorts of parties, games, activities, outings, and the like. These have their value. They are good in themselves. It is not good for man or woman to be left all alone. To be a hermit or a recluse is always a rare and very special vocation. But we don't want to let all the remaining precious hours of life be swallowed up by diversions. Nor do we want to let the hours weigh heavy or empty. We can fill them with great meaning. Through Scripture, through prayer, through faith-sharing we can increase our longing for the things of God (among them our faith and our hope), longings for ourselves and for the world. Our days can be filled with most efficacious prayer.

The Church has always had a great esteem for the contemplative vocation. Speaking under the inspiration of the Holy Spirit at the Second Vatican Council, Mother Church has said: "Communities which are entirely dedicated to contemplation, so that their members in solitude and silence, with constant prayer and penance willingly undertaken, occupy themselves with God alone, retain at all times, no matter how pressing the needs of the active apostolate may be, an honorable place in the Mystical Body of Christ, whose 'members do not all have the same function' (Rom. 12:4). For these offer to God a sacrifice of praise which is outstanding. Moreover the manifold results of their holiness lends luster to the people of God which is inspired by their example and which gains new members by their apostolate which is as effective as it is hidden. Thus they are revealed to be a glory of the Church and a wellspring of heavenly graces" (*Decree on the Renewal of Religious Life*, No. 7).

Those who have had a long, active, fruitful vocation in the world are often offered in their declining years a second (or a third or fourth) "career" — vocation — the powerful and meaningful vocation of the contemplative at the heart of the Church and the world. The Church has always had very few contemplatives, but she needs many, especially in these times, to pray and intercede for her children, tried by so many tribulations. As life lengthens, the Lord offers to more and more seniors the grace and the opportunity of serving the Church in this very important role.

If one accepts this beautiful invitation from the Lord and lives it, like Anna he or she will welcome the Lord with great joy and contentment whenever he comes. In the meantime such a senior will fill his or her days with great meaning, fulfilling an important role in the healing and salvation of the world, bringing peace to our earth.

When we go to church next Candlemas, we probably will not be carrying a candle. But we can bring something infinitely more precious — not the labor of our hands, but our very selves, the Christ who dwells in us. And giving ourselves again to God, we can let him bless us and illuminate us and send us back to the world as the Light of Christ, the Light of his People. By our prayer, by our love, by our presence, by our warmth, we can make Christ more present in this world, until it is time for us to sing our *Nunc Dimittis* and go our way in great peace, knowing that till the very end we have lived very meaningful lives and have been a source of life.

The Rosary

In 1977 I published my first book on prayer. It came about through the sagacity and kindness of a wonderful human being. John Delaney was in his last year as editor of Doubleday. His uncanny ability to spot and call forth Catholic writers had promoted Doubleday into being the foremost Catholic publisher in America. He had heard about my conferences on Centering Prayer and asked for a copy of them. While I was on a six-month retreat on Mount Athos he turned my conferences into a book. On my return I was greeted with the first copy of *Daily We Touch Him*. I was delighted, to say the least, and sent copies to all my relatives and friends. By this time Aunt Marion had retired to Florida with her husband, Skip, after a very successful career in the legal department of the telephone company. Aunt Marion wrote me a most heartening letter, telling me she had read the book from cover to cover and evidently thoroughly enjoyed it. But after all was said and done she concluded, "I'll stick with the rosary."

Some might be inclined to conclude, "Aunt Marion is old-fashioned." But they are wrong. The rosary is in! I have had innumerable young men in their late teens and early twenties ask me to teach them how to say the beads. Their parents' generation, who had learned the rosary at their mother's knee or in First Communion class, had left the beads behind and had never passed this bit of our Catholic heritage on to their children. But the young are interested in the beads.

One day a couple of years ago I was walking along the street in Columbus, Ohio, with a Salesian brother. Suddenly we heard a clatter behind us. As we turned around we found four breathless young girls running up to us. Three of them chimed in together that they were teaching their companion the rosary and they couldn't remember the fourth glorious mystery. Then they spotted

Father. I had to reflect a moment to remember the decade myself. They went off happy and giggling as they chanted: Assumption, Assumption. . . .

I have often said to my parish priest friends, if they put in the bulletin TONIGHT AT SEVEN IN THE PARISH HALL — INSTRUCTION ON THE USE OF CATHOLIC PRAYER BEADS, they would have a sellout crowd. The beads are in!

I hope if you have the joy of being a grandparent or great aunt or uncle you keep a spare rosary in the house and when your little relatives come to visit, you take the opportunity to share with them this treasure of the Church. Children have a special openness to grandparents and the like. You can be a wonderful link in the living tradition of the Church. When you place the beads in that little one's hands you don't know how far-reaching the effect will be. Just look back on your own life and see how often the rosary has been your companion in sorrow, your great comfort and strength. I have a most wonderful friend, a great man of prayer, a contemplative of the first order. But when I have been called to his side in the great crises of his life, each time I have found him with the rosary in hand. At such moments a child needs his mother and at such moments we are all children.

As you place the rosary in a little one's hands you give him or her a companion for life, and in death. And who knows — they may well pass it on to another generation and yet another generation. We are all part of the living tradition, and the rosary is an important part of that Catholic tradition.

Prayer with the rosary involves the whole person. As our sense of touch feels the beads passing through our fingers, our ears hear the cadence of the words, or at least the inner ear hears the inner voice. The mind is engaged in pondering the basic mysteries of our Catholic faith and our imaginations are put to work to support this with their ability to depict the scenes of salvation. Our hearts are called forth and our wills respond with appropriate resolutions. In the end our whole being cries: "Hail, holy Queen," and with her as our mediatrix we pray: "O God, pour forth your grace into our hearts, that we to whom the incarnation of your Son was made known by the message of an angel, may by his passion and death be brought to the glory of his resurrection."

This simple but rich way of praying, which Mary herself has so often endorsed, meets us wherever we might be on the journey of prayer. It brings us into contact with the basic teachings of our faith, giving us a good space in which to reflect on them again and again so that they can yield up the nourishment and meaningfulness for life that they contain. They put on our lips the basic prayers of our faith; and through repetition these prayers open out to us more and more. They become most truly the prayer of our hearts. They have formed our hearts. They have nourished our faith and hope. They begin to be constants on our lips. They form us to constant prayer. But then there are the days when we are just plain weary — be it weariness of body or of soul — just too weary to pray. Yet even then we can take our rosary in hand and just let it be our prayer while we rest in the Lord and in the loving care of his Mother.

In her last years when my mother was confined more and more to her apartment by crippling arthritis, she used to sit by the window that overlooked the entrance to the hospital where my brother ministered to the sick. In a way she would be watching for him to emerge and come to her. But at the same time her hands would be on her beads and she would pray for each one who entered or left the doors of the hospital, especially those who were rushed into the emergency entrance. She witnessed a lot of the drama of life from her window and made her contribution to it by her outreaching love and constant prayer. Mother one day said to me, "I wonder why it takes me so long to get through the beads. Some days it takes me all of twelve hours." If I told Mom that it was because she was enjoying a more contemplative type of prayer she would have pooh-poohed me. She was just a simple woman. Her whole life had been

that of a housewife and mother. She was
no contemplative. But the fact of the
matter is that the rosary leads those who
pray it regularly into a very simple and
contemplative type of prayer that hides
humbly beneath the oft-repeated words.
The rosary is a great school of prayer. It
can lead us all the way into the deepest
mysteries of our faith, into the depths of
that divine love that has revealed itself,
above all in the mysteries with which
the rosary puts us in touch. This
repeated reflection on the goodness and
compassion of our God cannot but
captivate our hearts and give us a deep
sense of hope and peace.

For many of us one of the happier
memories of our childhood is the family
rosary. It was perhaps there that we
learned the beads as we tried to keep up
with older brothers and sisters. How
good it was, all the family together,
peacefully praying, knowing the security
of being with one another in the loving
care of family, earthly and heavenly, for
at the center of the group was Mary in
her statue, a real presence. But there
were other ways and other days. I

remember one evening being in the home of a wealthy Catholic family. We were just completing a rather sumptuous meal. It had been most joyful with the nine children gathered around the table. As we were finishing dessert the youngest got up and went over to the server. He came back with what looked like a cigar box. The finishing touch. But, no. When he opened it, it revealed perhaps two dozen rosaries, each in its own little compartment. He made the round of the table and each took one. Then we concluded the meal with this beautiful prayer. With growing teenagers, it was the only way to get the family together for the family rosary. This family had another beautiful practice. Each took a turn leading a decade and the leader did not just announce the mystery but offered his or her own little reflection on it.

Of course, as time marches on, the members of a family go on to find their own way in the world and to begin their own families. Soon only Mom and Dad remain, and perhaps only Mom or Dad.

I don't think we have to abandon the family rosary even then. True, it won't be quite the same, but there is no reason why each evening the head of the house cannot in spirit gather in all the members from wherever they may be (here in this world of pilgrimage or from beyond, closer to Mary now) and together again in spirit make the rounds of the beads. The power of a loving heart makes a presence before the Lord as powerful as any physical presence. As the saying goes, the family that prays together stays together — even when the miles separate.

One time in life when all Catholics instinctively reach for the beads is in "the hour of our death." When perhaps the mind has become too confused to put any coherent words together, when perhaps the lips are too parched to utter a word or the body too frail to empower a sound, the fingers can yet feel. We hold the beads tightly. The rosary in our hands silently proclaims our faith in all its mysteries, our faith in the unfailing mediation of Mother Mary. It is a bond with the world beyond, our passport. It will not let our hand slip from Mary's in overwhelming weakness. It is our silent, unceasing prayer, the prayer that is now to be fulfilled in its completeness: "Be with us now and in the hour of our death." We may have often slipped away, and even gone very far off like the prodigal son, but now our rosary says we are children of heaven and want to return to our Father's house. And with Mary mediating, our Father hurries out to meet us and orders for us that fine garment and that heavenly feast.

As we finally lay at peace in our coffin, the rosary is there, still in our hands. It is a powerful witness to a lifetime of struggling with prayer, trying to have a meaningful and faithful relationship with God. It proclaims to all who approach that we have to the end believed in the saving mysteries that each decade unfolds. It tells of our undying confidence in Mary, which is now fulfilled, for she has prayed for us at the hour of our death and seen us safe home. And as those who have loved us kneel about our coffin and pray again the beads, they find the strength and consolation they need to go on without us. I know it well and so do you, for we have all prayed the rosary at the coffin of others so dear to us. Mary is life, sweetness, and hope.

Aunt Marion is sticking to the rosary, and I am very happy about that. I only hope that when she fingers those beads she doesn't forget her nephew. I am sure she doesn't!

In His Steps

Dreams do come true. Many have for me over the years. But perhaps one of the most precious and beautiful for me was that of walking in our Lord's footsteps in the Holy Land. I had ten beautiful days there. Bible in hand, I went to Nazareth and Capernaum, Tabor and Jericho, Bethlehem and Jerusalem. Each place I read again of our Lord's doings, I listened to his words. I looked out on the scene he beheld. I waded in his sea. I felt the burning heat of his desert. I experienced his long treks along the hot dusty roads. I mingled with the crowds in the bazaars. I heard the mournful chant at David's tomb and by the wall. I bowed my head against the stone and prayed with Jesus. I prostrated under the olive trees and tried to let my heart be attentive to his Spirit and to his prayer.

While I was in Jerusalem I was privileged to stay with the Sisters of

Sion at the Second Station of the Cross. The Sisters gave me a small room at the very top of their house, really on the roof, apart from all the others. From my room I could look out over the vast expanse of the Temple area, now dominated by a great mosque, the Dome of the Rock, and then out across the crowded old city with its many church towers, domes, and minarets. Regularly the cry would go out from the mullahs, summoning the sons of Allah to their prayers; and again the *Angelus* bell would invite the followers of Jesus to recall that act central in all of sacred history: the coming of God to be one with us in our humanity.

The first call to prayer in the morning came from the minarets at about four in the morning. It seemed as if the minaret of the great mosque in the Temple area were in direct line with my small room. Each morning I would be almost physically cast out of my bed with the loudly broadcast cry of the mullah. I had no objections, though. I could rise and soon be on my way to Calvary before the streets and the basilica became crowded with pilgrims and tourists.

My journey began in what was really the basement of the convent of the Sisters of Sion. There, still exposed to our eyes and our feet, were the very paving stones upon which our Lord stood as he was condemned to death and took up his cross. From there the Way of the Cross is not particularly marked out, but the lay of these ancient streets (or at least their narrow confines) probably has not altered much since that day when the soldiers hurried our Savior toward the ancient city gate and the hillock outside. Many of the stations are marked solely with a Roman numeral painted on the façade of the building that presses on the street. At the fourth station there is a little chapel, not much more than a niche in the wall, with a statue of the sorrowing Mother. The Little Sisters of Charles de Foucauld now live at the seventh station, and the front of their little house folds open to share their chapel or prayer room with those making the *Via Dolorosa*. The old gate is gone now; the city has grown out repeatedly to embrace more and more of the surroundings. The great basilica of the Savior is totally engulfed in a sea of tightly packed buildings, residences, and shops. Indeed, a whole monastic community now resides on its roof in little huts.

When I first entered the basilica, coming up the back way, following the Way of the Cross, I could get no perspective of the great building and, once within, no sense of where Calvary itself was. The most sacred hill is not prominent in the great church but rather stands almost hidden and crowded in one corner, not far from the main door. Steps lead up the twenty or so feet to the small sanctuary. Beneath the altar one can reach down into a hole and touch the sacred rock. Nearby it is possible to offer Mass as I did on a number of mornings.

But what is really central in the basilica, the focus of all, is the tomb — the empty tomb of our Lord. Perhaps we have the tendency to center too much on the hill in the corner. We linger too long where Christ lingered only three hours.

He stayed longer in the tomb, but even that was short — a very short three days. And then he left it empty. This is the center of Jerusalem, the center of our religion, of our faith: ". . . if Christ has not been raised [from the dead], then our preaching is in vain and your faith is in vain" (1 Corinthians 15:14). Our journey never ends here. We go out from here, like our Master, to walk among men and women, and then to ascend to heavenly places.

Catholic tradition invites us to spend time walking in this Way of the Cross. Some churches, unfortunately, have been stripped of the stations, others have relegated them to some out-of-the-way place. Most, in their renovations, have replaced the old tableaux. Perhaps that is good. It leaves us more open to enter into the mystery of the mysteries. Even if we cannot go to church, we can walk this way with the Lord, perhaps holding in our hands a cross especially blessed for this. It is a journey we frequently want to make.

Each time we walk this way with our Lord, it is in fact a different journey.

Each time, if we remain attentive, he leads us into other aspects of the mystery of salvation; he speaks to us where we are. Take, for example, the fourth station, one that is most important for me. Some days, as I meet Mary there, I am very conscious how she is always with me on this journey — on the journey of life. Her love, her concern, her care, and her support surround me. I am never left alone on the journey. Other days her presence makes me realize how much others suffer because of my sufferings, and this increases them, just as her suffering must have increased those of her beloved Son. Sometimes meeting Mary there makes me realize how much others are with me on the way, how much I am loved, that there are those who will go all the way on the journey with me. I am consoled, strengthened, and encouraged. I recall, too, at times, how Mary went all the way with Jesus — for me! She is, as some theologians have called her, Co-redemptrix. With Jesus she freely offered that most sacred life to the Father for my sins. As Mother, the

98

source of his human life, she had a certain claim on it. And freely she offered it and let go of it on this horrendous altar of sacrifice. When she said "yes" that quiet, awesome day in Nazareth she probably had no idea where it would lead — that it would lead to this. We say our "yes" to the Lord, encouraged by her courage, not knowing where it might lead, but knowing for a certainty that wherever that may be, she will be there, and we will be upheld by all the graces of his and her most blessed passion. And in the end, it will always lead to an empty tomb. Because of his empty tomb, her tomb was emptied, and so will ours be.

The daily quiet walking, at least in the spirit, of this sacred Way of the Cross, can be one of the great graces in our lives. As we go along we touch the deepest mysteries, and our faith is enlivened. We see how much we are loved, and we have ample cause for hope. Whose love will not grow in the experience of such love? All our emotions can flow and we can experience a great release. Our little sufferings take perspective and meaning. And at the end there is always ultimate meaning, the empty tomb — resurrection and ascension — for Christ and for each one of us, his members.

Lent leads to Easter, its whole meaning. Without Easter, there would be no Lent. Life leads to heaven, its whole meaning. Without heaven, there is no true life. We are on a journey, and like any journey, it would be meaningless if it did not have a destination. But it does have a destination, a wonderful, glorious, assured destination. The way thereto has been opened to us by this sorrowful journey to Calvary; it has been assured to us by this journey. The Way of the Cross underlines the meaning of all life, even as it gives meaning to the little — and the greater — sufferings and crosses of life. May the special grace of the stations be a renewed experience of this.

Hearing the Word of God

". . . A woman in the crowd raised up her voice and said to him: 'Blessed is the womb that bore you, and the breasts that you sucked!' But he said, 'Blessed rather are those who hear the word of God and keep it!' " (Luke 11:27-28).

Jesus, in his response, certainly was not contradicting this woman who undoubtedly knew the joy of motherhood. To be the mother of such a Man! Both what she cried out and what Jesus responded are in praise of the Virgin Mother. Mary was certainly blessed in having such a Son and being able to nurture him at the breast. What intimacy with God! But it was through hearing and accepting the word of God — as it was brought to her through the Scriptures she had listened to all her life, through the living tradition of her people, God's Chosen People, and ultimately through the messenger of God, the angel Gabriel — that she became the very Mother of Christ-God. It was through such hearing and keeping the word that Mary not only fulfilled perfectly her role as Mother of God but also mothered the Christ in herself and in all of us. By living such a life of living faith Mary became the first of our Lord's disciples, the mother and model for all who live by faith.

Scripture, the revealing word of God, always has many levels of meaning. While the text here speaks first of Mary and Christ Jesus, it speaks also of Mother Church and of each one of us who have been born into Christ in the Church.

Mother Church, the new People of God, is blessed in bearing each of us into Christ through the womb of the font. We are born into Christ, made his living members, one with him our head, through the sacrament of baptism. Our Lord comes again and lives in this world in us his members, as we are called upon to "complete what is lacking in Christ's afflictions" (Colossians 1:24).

Mother Church nourishes us on the breasts of the Eucharist. The most nourishing food conceivable, it makes us ever more fully alive in Christ.

It is our responsibility to go on hearing the word of God and keeping it, living by it. We are to hear it at the Liturgy of the Word when we go to be nourished at the Eucharist. Each time we gather with our sisters and brothers for Mass, the Lord is there in the voice of his mothering Church to speak to us a particular, personal word, the word of God we need at that moment to hear — if we would but listen with the ears of faith.

We are to hear the saving and nourishing word also in the sanctuary of our own homes, of our own rooms — whether it be in the "liturgy of the family" or in the solitude of our own space. I know a family, actually a retired couple. As they sit down to their frugal breakfast each morning, they first feed their souls, their Christ-life. After the morning offering, one reads a psalm and then the other a passage from the Gospels. They can't make the journey to the parish church anymore; it is a bit too far for weary, faltering old limbs, but they still need and get their daily bread.

Later in the day you might find one or the other of them sitting by the window, getting the warmth of the sun and the fullness of the light, Bible on lap, gently "chewing" on the word of God. The Bible is always on their coffee table so it is easy to take a "bite" now and then. They keep well nourished, and growing — growing in spirit, growing in Christ, even though the body may be in decline.

We are told that "Mary kept all these things, pondering them in her heart" (Luke 2:19). She let the wonders that God was accomplishing in her life and among his people — beyond understanding though they be — stand quietly in her heart. This is the deepest prayer of presence and wonder. It is easy to pray Mary's way: We are just there with what is, what the word of God tells us. We are nourished, and truly blessed.

This kind of growth and development need never end, no matter how many years we might claim. We can go on and on, nourishing the Christ in us — and in others, sharing with them what we have pondered in our hearts.

Blessed are they who hear the word of God, keep it in their own hearts, and share it with others.

Tree Care
(Or How to Make
Our Lives Fruitful)

Have you ever thought of yourself as a fig tree?

One day Jesus did call us fig trees, at least that is the image he chose for us in one of his parables: "A man [God the Father] had a fig tree [you and me] planted in his vineyard; and he came seeking fruit on it and found none. And he said to the vinedresser [Jesus], 'Lo, these three years I have come seeking fruit on this fig tree, and I find none. Cut it down; why should it use up the ground?' And he answered, 'Let it alone, sir, this year also, till I dig about it and put on manure. And if it bears fruit next year, well and good; but if not, you can cut it down" (Luke 13:6-9).

I think many of us look upon our lives as largely fruitless. Even when we have apparently accomplished a great deal and others acclaim our doings, deep down inside we feel hollow. Indeed, it is often at moments of acclamation that we most sense the fruitlessness of our lives. This comes, I think, from two sources. First, we are conscious of all the largesse of God, of all the graces and blessings we have received, of all the potential he has given us. In comparison with this, we have accomplished virtually nothing. Then, too, we know it is not our doings that really matter. These are so extrinsic to ourselves. It is our being that counts. Through the years — three is an infinite number; it can stand for any number of years, all the years of our lives — we have not really expressed in life our own magnificence, the magnificence of a person who is made to the image of God himself and has been baptized into the very life and being of the Son, a partaker of the divine life and nature. We remember our Lord's words at the Last Supper about his Father wanting us to bear fruit and bear it abundantly. We want to do that, we want to do something about it.

But what can we do?

In his parable, our Lord tells us what we can do. We can let him open space in our lives so that we can get in touch with our magnificence and we can let him pile on his nourishing "manure," the "fertilizer" of life.

To paraphrase the Psalmist: "Be still, and know that I am God." It is when we fulfill this injunction that we open space in our lives with the Lord. We need to sit quietly and let go of all our own thoughts and images and feelings, and listen to the sounds of silence, listen to the Lord present within us. Centering Prayer is a very simple, traditional method for doing this:

Centering Prayer

Sit relaxed and quiet.

1. Be in faith and love to God who dwells in the center of your being.
2. Take up a love word and let it be gently present, supporting your being to God in faith-filled love.
3. Whenever you become *aware* of

anything else, simply, gently,
return to the Lord with the use of
your prayer word.

At the end of the prayer (usually
twenty minutes) let the Our Father (or
some other prayer) pray itself within.

This is only one way of doing this.
You may have another. The way we do it
is not the important thing. The
important thing is that we do take time
to be still with the Lord and let him
open the spaces within so that we can be
in touch with our own true beauty and
being in him.

Then we need to let him "spread
manure" over us, to "fertilize" us. If we
are city folk, we are apt to think of
manure as something quite repulsive:
dirty, smelly waste that one decidedly
docs not want around. Thus, when our
Lord speaks of manure we might
immediately think of the trials that are
heaped upon us. These can indeed be a
great source of grace when we bear with
them in the right way. But I do not think
that is what our Lord is talking about
here. He comes from an agricultural

society, one close to the soil and very organic in its approach to life. No farmer will ever look down on manure. For him, it is pure gold. He knows there is nothing better to get his crops to grow and bear fruit abundantly. The smell is pure fragrance.

The manure we want to let the Lord heap upon us is his word of life. The just person lives by faith, and faith comes from hearing. It is from hearing the word of God that we are made fruitful. We need to make space in our lives daily to hear the word of God and let it seep down deep into our being.

Again we have a simple, traditional method to do this. It is called *Lectio Divina*, or contemplative reading:

Lectio Divina

1. Take the Sacred Text with reverence, acknowledging God's presence, and call upon the Holy Spirit.
2. For ten minutes listen to the Lord and respond to him.
3. Thank the Lord and take a "word" with you.

If each day we make some time for Centering Prayer and *Lectio Divina* we are doing our part to allow the Man who looks after the vineyard to do what needs to be done so that we may be fruitful fig trees. The Lord fully respects us. He respects our freedom, for he knows it is the greatest thing he has given us — it is our power to choose and to love. He will never force himself upon us. But if we give him the space, by Centering Prayer and *Lectio*, to act in our lives, then he will open the soil around us and manure us so that we may bear abundant fruit. As Saint Paul said, "I planted, Apollos watered, but God gave the growth" (1 Corinthians 3:6). We sow the word of God within by *Lectio*. We water the roots by Centering. And then the Lord will send coursing through us that sap of grace which will make us bear abundant fruit.

No longer will the Master of the vineyard say, "Cut it down." Rather will he say: "This is my beloved in whom I am well pleased." Let us be fruitful trees. Let us learn and practice good tree care.

What About the Liturgy?

The liturgy is not a mere act of memory, recalling events that happened many centuries ago. It is a reliving of the events of salvation history. They are made truly present in us with all their saving power. These events that did take place historically in a particular moment of our human time exist eternally in the NOW of God. And in the liturgy we, as it were, reach into that NOW of God and bring these very same events back into our time and into our lives.

Our time is like a great passing train. Event after event passes by. And as we stand at our particular station in life, we experience one event after the other. But God stands at the summit of creation. All is immediately present to him and in him in his eternal NOW.

Take the Mass, for instance. The

absolute supreme moment in all of creation was that moment when the Son of God, become man, offered to his Father the greatest thing in all of creation: his own life. When the Christian community gathers to celebrate the ritual act of the Mass, we reach into God's eternal NOW and bring forth that supreme moment and make it again present in the course of our time. There is absolutely no difference between what happened in the Supper Room and on Calvary and what takes place on our altars. Each is a temporal presence of the one supreme act of sacrificial and salvific love.

So, too, in all the liturgy. As we walk through Holy Week, each of the moments of the week is made present on our earth in liturgical sacrament, present with all the power to save and heal and glorify the Father that it had the first time it was made present in Jerusalem. We are invited to be present at these events — or rather, as the Christ-community, to make them present.

In baptism we were baptized into

Christ. We were made one with him in a oneness that is truly beyond our comprehension. It will be a thing of wonder for us for all eternity — how we are so completely one with the very Son of God. Christ lives now in this world in us. As we in the Church-community relive these saving mysteries of Christ, we make them present in ourselves in this world now for the salvation of this world.

Saint Paul has what was for me a very mysterious saying: We are to "complete what is lacking in Christ's afflictions" (Colossians 1:24). How can anything be wanting in the passion of Christ? Christ's act of saving love was totally sufficient to save this world and every other imaginable world besides. It is an act of infinite meaning, beauty, and efficacy. In it there can be nothing lacking. What is lacking is its historical presence in our world here and now. This is what lies in wait for us to do. By being Christ in the historical world of today, letting him live out his passion in us now, we with him make his passion with all its saving power immediately

114

present to ourselves and to all our brothers and sisters.

This being so, let us be who we truly are, both as individuals baptized into Christ and as the Christ-community, and fully enter into the Christ-mystery in its liturgical celebration, making present our Savior's life and mission. Let us try, insofar as our life situation and vocation allows us, to be who we most truly are. Let us not be afraid to turn off the television and lay aside the newspapers and magazines, forgo some of our usual social events and interactions, and, as much as possible, be in mind and spirit and body with the Christ-community.

Entering as fully as we can into these saving mysteries and letting them enter into us, and through us into our world, we will be able to enter most fully into their fruit, the risen life of our Lord Jesus. If we truly live in the fullness of our Christ-person, then we will indeed rise to a new level of being. The risen life will be more fully ours. We will know profoundly within ourselves its joy, its peace, and its reality.

This entering in is not altogether easy. Apart from the discipline of setting things aside and making space and giving ourselves to the community celebrations, we are confronted with certain confusing realities.

The words Jesus speaks during these days are often difficult for us to penetrate and understand. They were spoken to another time and people and place. The signs he uses are not those we employ in our everyday life, like the washing of the feet of a guest, so familiar to his times. The central act itself of this Holy Week is somewhat foreign to us. Sacrifice was certainly understandable to those people who day after day saw and offered sacrifices in the Temple. They even knew of human sacrifice among their neighbors and in their own history. Abraham was asked to sacrifice his own son. But sacrifice is quite foreign to us.

More profound and even more confusing is what is at the source of all this, the incomprehensibly gratuitous love of God. How humbling and baffling to us is this love. A love that knows no limits. A love that is not put off by all our ingratitude and sin. A love that goes to such lengths.

Yes, as we enter deeply into the liturgy, we have much cause for confusion. What are we to do? We can but live it and let it reveal itself to us in its own mysterious way. Saint Thomas Aquinas writes in his *Summa* of theology that where the mind leaves off, the heart goes on. It is time to leave off thinking and trying to figure things out and fit them all into the narrow confines of our intellects. It is time to live the mysteries and let them speak deeply to us through the intuitions of lived love.

I think of Mother Teresa of Calcutta. What she does is utterly incomprehensible to the Hindu mind. Collecting the dying from the streets and wasting time and energy and material goods on them is so contrary to their understanding of karma and the way life should be allowed to unfold. Yet, as they witness her labors, they intuitively comprehend her love and holiness. She is the saint of India today. And of the world. Even a paganized and

117

post-Christian world was impelled to lay at her feet its greatest tribute, the Nobel Peace Prize. And it was not for any great act of world diplomacy like the other recipients, but precisely for her being in love to these, the most deprived on the earth, the dying destitute.

In spite of ourselves, the perceptions of love are the most powerful — if we allow them space in our lives so that they can have their impact on us. This is why the Church-community goes step by step with our Lord in the liturgical celebration. As is chanted in the Byzantine liturgy, let us when we take part in the liturgy lay aside all earthly cares. Let us truly make it a holy time, with care and concern only for what truly matters. May we allow the reality of Christ-in-our-lives to be, and bring that reality to our world so that not only we ourselves but our whole human family may rise to a new level of being, life, and love. The more of us who do this, the more the passion of Christ will be filled up to the redemption and resurrection of all.

True Christian Greatness

We are privileged to live in a time of special grace. It is the time of an ecumenical council, when the Holy Spirit has been poured forth upon the human family in a very special way. In our days our Blessed Mother has been appearing on the earth. In many places the Church of Christ is suffering for and with him, standing with the poor and the oppressed. It is a time of saints and martyrs.

If I were to ask you, who do you think is the greatest saint on earth today, what would you answer? The wisest among us might say, "God knows," for the Lord has a way of hiding his greatest saints. But I think many of us would say Mother Teresa of Calcutta.

I was tremendously moved and amazed when the committee that

chooses the recipients of the Nobel Peace Prize chose Mother Teresa in 1984 to receive that honor. I was surprised and happy that they had the insight to see that the true way to peace is through profound respect for the human person, no matter how poor, weak, or underprivileged.

Mother Teresa stands before us, very much an incarnation of the Gospels, a proclamation of their truest meaning. Especially does she exemplify those words of the Lord that we find in Matthew: ". . . whoever would be great among you must be your servant, and whoever would be first among you must be your slave" (20:26-27). She chose the place of service among the lowest, the last, and the least. And it was not easy.

Mother Teresa herself tells us that the hardest thing she had to do was to leave her dear Loretto. She had spent eighteen happy years with other nuns, her sisters in the Lord. She had served, teaching the daughters of the affluent, living securely in a fine convent. But out her window she could see the neighboring slums. In 1946 the Lord spoke to her about a more radical greatness. In 1947 she saw those slums swell as the partition between India and Pakistan brought, literally, millions to the slums of Calcutta. In August of 1948 she courageously stepped out of the convent security and went to dwell and labor among the poorest and most needy. Her departure was not made any easier by the fact that many of the nuns and many lay people and ecclesiastics whom she respected shook their heads and decried the fact that Sister Teresa was being unfaithful to her vows, putting off her habit (the sari she adopted is simply the common garb of Indian women), and going to do "her own thing." Mother Teresa had to believe deep in her own heart that what she was about was God's thing, not hers. She was obeying the Gospel.

Should we as Christians aspire to greatness, to being first? I think the answer to that question is a "yes" and a "no." We are great. We are made in the very image of God. We are the children of God. We have been Christed in baptism, made partakers of the divine life and nature. This is our call, and we should live up to it. But we can seek only true greatness, Christ's greatness: ". . . the Son of man came not to be served but to serve" (Matthew 20:28).

However, if we go forth to serve only to obtain our own greatness, that is not right. That is not truly serving; it is self-serving. We must forget ourselves and go out of ourselves in compassion. It is the way of compassion. It is the way of Christ, who emptied himself and became like us and suffered all we suffer, save sin.

I think there are two kinds of needs we can respond to and two motivations we can be conscious of; but, in fact, they all come together into one — in being a Christ-person.

There is the passionate love of our Lord that sees him in others, especially the poor and needy, and joyfully responds to his need there. This is the way and the need that stands out in Mother Teresa's life and mission.

When I was in Calcutta, I had the privilege of offering Mass at the novitiate of the Missionaries of Charity and of speaking at length with Mother Teresa, who told me on that occasion that she demands a twofold conversion on the part of her novices before they can be professed as Missionaries of Charity. First, there is the conversion required of every religious: one must turn his or her back on the ambitions, the power, and the pleasures of a worldly life and embrace the evangelical counsels in their full expression. Then, during their later novitiate, Mother Teresa herself tries to lead the aspirants through another conversion experience. They go out in the early morning to pick up the old and dying who have been abandoned during the night, the most wretched human misery. The novices bring them home and care for them; afterward they meditate and pray and offer Mass in the light of their experience, seeking to come into the fullness of the Christ-mystery here until they do come to realize that it is a *privilege* and *joy* to serve Christ in these, the most wretched. Only then are they ready to be professed as Missionaries of Charity, of Love.

123

Most of us, in our affluent society, in our settled ways of life, do not come into much contact with such need and misery. And most of us are not being called to leave all that we have and to go to the slums of New York or Port-au-Prince to be with the poorest and serve Christ in them. The mystical body of Christ has many members and there are many calls. But no matter where we are, we are surrounded by very real need and very real misery.

All about us, in our own homes, in our work areas, on the streets we walk, there are people who so much need love, care, concern, respect, and compassion. We all have our terrible wounds, our needs. We have our pains and hurts, our sins and our weaknesses. We have our false pride and pretense, our intolerance and prejudice, our self-righteousness and anger, our little cruelties, our indifference, our hardness of heart. These needs are all around us, and even in us. How can we respond to them in loving service?

First of all, we can pray — a most hidden but effective service. We can ask our Lord to enlighten and comfort those about us whom we see sinning, hurting themselves and others. And give them courage, when they see, to change and embrace the way of Christ's love.

Then we can be patient and compassionate. God is so patient with us all. He walks with us day by day as we grow and outgrow our stupidity and blindness and misery. We should be ready to walk with others. If we are honest with ourselves, we can look back and see how often we have done stupid and hurtful things — not because we wanted to, not because we were malicious, but simply because we did not see, did not understand, what we were doing. If we continue to grow, next year we will be able to see how even today we are missing the boat in so many ways. Knowing ourselves in honesty we cannot but be compassionate, entering into the hurts and blindness of others.

Another important ministry is that of affirmation, of praise. We are so prone to see first — in ourselves and in others — the sins, the failures, the weaknesses.

We miss the doughnut for seeing the hole. We do not see the wonderful child of God, the image of God, who is there, failing though she or he may be. We can never praise one another too much, for we can never praise the very image of God too much. In affirming others' goodness, we give them a chance to live out of that goodness, instead of out of their sin and failure.

Finally, and most difficult, there is fraternal correction. But note, it is *fraternal* correction. We can effectively correct others and call them forth only when they know we are loving brothers and sisters and that the correction is coming out of love for them, wanting to help them grow. Until they know that love, our attempts at correction will only alienate and often drive the sinner more into his or her sin. So this ministry is not something we will often be able to exercise.

But there will always be room for prayer, praise, and patience. We can always bring compassion, care, and consolation. This is Christian greatness, to be with others in their need, and let that need bite into our own souls, even when it is sin and misery. He, Christ Jesus, took on the burden of our sin. We can pass on all our burdens to him and be Christ with the sinner in compassion. There is no one who cannot minister and thus attain to true greatness.

Are We Laughing?

For me, one of the great blessings the Lord has given us through the Second Vatican Council has been the renewal of the liturgy. Not just the use of the vernacular and the simplification and variety introduced into the Mass and the other rites, but especially the rich lectionary. Each day we have two or three different readings through a two-year cycle. The first reading is taken from the Old Testament and the last from the Gospels. It has been fascinating for me to see how the spiritual meanings of these two texts have brought each other forth. I have carried this over into my own daily reading. As I read a text from the Old Testament, if it reminds me of one in the New, I turn to that and listen to them together.

The other day I was reading that beautiful passage from Chapter 18 of Genesis where God came to Abraham's tent in the form of three strangers — the first hint of the revelation of the Trinity. Abraham and Sarah, no youngsters then, hurried about preparing a meal for the three in whom they saw God. After the meal was laid out, in the midst of their enjoyment, God revealed to Abraham the good news he had come to bring. Next time he would pass that way, he said, in the very next year, Abraham's sterile wife, now not far from a hundred years of age, would be pregnant. Sarah, who was inside the tent at that moment, laughed when she overheard this promise, saying: "My husband over a hundred and me at my age, am I to have a child?" The Lord had appeared to Abraham many times and had promised that he and Sarah would parent a great family that would be God's Chosen People and a nation among nations. The fulfillment of this couple's hopeless hope reminded me of another couple.

On the third day after Jesus had died on the cross and was buried in a stranger's tomb, two men trudged downhill from Jerusalem toward Emmaus. Jesus came alongside of them, but neither of them had the perception of Abraham to see the Lord in the stranger. They related the cause of their sadness: a hope that had failed. They had followed Jesus. They told the stranger about Jesus and all that had happened, concluding with one of the saddest statements in Scripture: ". . . we *had hoped* that he was the one to redeem Israel" (Luke 24:21; author's emphasis).

A hope that has fallen into past tense is one of the great sorrows of human life.

Jesus, the Stranger, began to open the Scriptures for them, and then, in a communion meal, they recognized him in the breaking of the bread. They realized that their hearts had begun to burn again with hope as he opened the Scriptures for them. Recognizing him, they rushed out to share with others the good news and what they had experienced. The Lord is risen, indeed.

In both of these instances, God came to a couple on a journey, the journey of life, after their hope had faded. The Lord comes to us, today, each day. He tells us we can be saints, we can be fulfilled, we can make a difference, we can be a source of life for others, parenting, even in our old age. Do we, like Sarah, laugh — to mock an extinguished hope? Do we think the time for fruitfulness is over? Do we say, "We had hoped"?

Can we hope again?

Jesus, the Stranger — has he become a stranger to us? — shows us how we can refind our hope and become fruitful, even in old age. We can let him join us on the journey. We can take up our Bibles and listen, humbly, eagerly, and let him open the word of God to us and enkindle hope in our hearts once again. We can join the community of believers in the breaking of the bread and let him renew our experience of faith. Then we can proclaim to all about us and all with whom we come into contact and all whom we write and call: Jesus is indeed risen. In him, we, too, shall arise. We have life. We have hope. We have eternal life.

What matter if we are ninety years, or a hundred? We can give birth to new life in all whom we meet — a life that will last forever. How many around us would say, "We had hoped"? How many never had any hope that went beyond this very limited life? We, in the warmth of the love we allow the Lord to enkindle in our hearts through his revelation, can reach out and engender true hope and life in others, no matter what our age. We can make a difference. We can parent a life that will last forever. We need never say, "We had hoped." We can hope, every day of our lives, to make a difference, as we share with others the good news, that Jesus Christ is Lord, a risen Lord, and we, too, shall rise to eternal life. Amen. Alleluia!

We have ample cause to laugh — with purest joy!

A Mother's Power

"On the third day there was a marriage at Cana in Galilee, and the mother of Jesus was there" (John 2:1).

Mary was now what our society would call a "senior citizen." She was a widow, cared for by the social provisions of her society, provisions perhaps much more human, familial, and warm than ours. The extended family gathered around, and cared for their widows. They would always enjoy a place of honor in the family and fulfill their traditional roles.

When the family gathered at Cana for the marriage of two of their young ones, Mary was there in her extended role of mother. Her Son, Jesus, was there, too. He had now come into the fullness of his manhood and had entered into a position of particular power in their society — he was a teaching rabbi with a band of dedicated disciples. He possessed a magnetic power that drew men and women. Yet he had still greater powers of which others were not yet aware. None but his mother knew.

A pressing social need arose, at this wedding feast in Cana. A wedding had an importance that it is difficult for us to truly estimate today. The marriage celebration was the great moment in the life of every Jew. The whole of the extended family gathered and made their contribution. A failure in the completeness would cause common embarrassment, real disgrace for the family. It could have considerable impact on their social relations and even on their businesses. Even more, each wedding was a moment of importance for the whole of the People of the Promise. Every wedding served as a part of the Chosen People's preparation for the coming of the Messiah. The celebration expressed a confident hope — it was an anticipation of the great messianic celebration to come.

The matter was, then, of great importance. And of the greatest urgency. Mary, the mother, stepped in, and tapped the hidden source of power of which she was fully aware. At first the Son seemed unresponsive, almost rude. But the mother would not be put off. Mary knew not only her Son's power but the depths of his compassion and love — as only a mother would know them. We all know the results. This was the first sign that Jesus worked, here in Cana of Galilee.

A great social catastrophe weighs on our people today — the people of the whole world. One people now, in our global village, an extended family. And this catastrophe will not just embarrass, disgrace, hurt business, and fail to show support for the divine plan and promise. It might well utterly destroy us and terminate all promise for the human race. Day by day the nuclear arsenals grow. We are devouring our resources to produce monsters that must in the end be cared for on incalculably expensive scrap piles — at least that is where we hope they will end up. With the birth of each new monster the danger of "accidents" and actual fallout grows geometrically.

When we, and some of the best

economists with us, look at the present situation, we seem to be trapped in an armament economy. An enormous amount of our own national budget goes into arms — and most of the aid we give other countries, even some of the poorest, goes to them in the form of arms produced in United States factories. Millions and millions of jobs depend on the arms race. Yet there does lie in the hands of American industrial power — ultimately those of the leaders of the multinationals, but even in the hands of small-business executives and middle management — the power to begin to create a shift and show that there are viable economic alternatives. The immense genius that has created the colossus of war and destruction certainly can create an economy of peace: cleaning up our cities and depressed areas, working out effective food distribution so there will be no hunger and no waste, creating truly productive job programs for the millions of idle hands around the world, and making electricity affordable and good water available for all. The genius is here, but not the political will, yet. If only a small amount of the research monies and the efforts of the think-tanks were turned in this new direction, if only even a few of the small companies would show what can be done, they could serve as the hidden little rudder that would change the course of the mighty ship of world economy.

The men who can make the decisions to create this lifesaving rudder have mothers. These mothers know their sons' power and are proud of it. And they know, too, the deep roots of compassion and love that they have nurtured in their boys. Let them use their maternal influence to bring this desperate need to their sons' attention. Like Mary, let them not be put off if the initial response seems cool or is even a rebuff. But let them go on to press the cause that can save the world.

We owe everything to mothers (and fathers). May they mother the world — with Mary's help and grace — and bring it to a saving order of peace.

Be Like Our Mother

One of the ways for us to get more into the Scriptures and obtain a fuller understanding of them is to enter into them as one of the characters in the particular scene we are considering. Returning to the Annunciation story (see Luke 1:26-38) I would like to suggest that you be Mary. It is not out of place. After all, she is our mother and we are like her in all but sin — she had none of it, we have plenty.

Can you imagine how flabbergasted Mary was when an angel came winging into her room — or however he arrived? Can you imagine how you would react if an angel suddenly showed up in your room? And as if that wasn't enough, the heavenly visitor went on to greet her: "Hail, full of grace." Not "Hail, Mary," but some almost incomprehensible and exalted title.

When she got by this — and she needed a little angelic assurance to manage it: "Fear not, Mary [it must have been reassuring to hear him use her own name], you have found favor with God. God is happy with you, don't worry." A very nice thing to hear! — she had yet to face the burden of his message, what he was asking of her: to become pregnant (an unwed mother in such a closed society!), to become pregnant with God, to bring God and salvation to her people!

By God's grace she said "yes." In her humility, she said "yes." That is the keynote here — humility.

It takes a lot of humility to accept true greatness. We can manage a little greatness, because we can think it comes from us. But true greatness — *that* cannot come from us. We know it. We know the truth. And that is humility — knowing and accepting the truth. We had rather flatter ourselves with our little doings than accept the humiliation of being truly great.

When Mary said "yes," she said it as our mother. She did it to give us an example and to get us the grace to do likewise.

Today, now, God summons each of us to what is indeed flabbergasting: to be truly his son or daughter and Mary's, to be one with the Son, and to save the entire human race, the world that is groaning for salvation. God invites us to stop pursuing our silly little greatnesses, to stop trying to do this or that well, to be a good homemaker, or teacher, or baker, or whatever according to our own images. God asks us now to be truly his son or daughter, to be open to live a complete "yes" as his Son did, as Mary did. "Behold the servant of the Lord; be it done unto me according to your word" — not mine — "not my will but yours be done."

He summons us to live love, that serving love that sent the newly pregnant mother across the hills to her cousin Elizabeth. To live the love of Jesus before the Father in the night so that we can live the love of Jesus among the brethren during the day, seeking only the things that please the Father. For this we cannot afford to have any preconceived notions or images. We have to let God at each moment of

140

each day and night call us forth to undeserved greatness, to be persons pregnant with God, bringing salvation to all his people. "Behold the servant of the Lord. . . ."

Be like our Mother — that is the challenge we hear and experience when we dare to enter into the Scriptures as Mary, our Mother.

A Prayer for Those Growing Old

Lord, you know I am growing older.

Keep me from becoming talkative and possessed with the idea that I must express myself on every subject.

Release me from the craving to straighten out everyone's affairs.

Keep me from the recital of endless detail. Give me wings to get to the point.

Seal my lips when I am inclined to tell of my aches and pains. They are increasing with the years, and my love to speak of them grows sweeter as time goes by.

Teach me the glorious lesson that occasionally I may be wrong. Make me thoughtful but not nosy, helpful but not bossy. With my vast store of wisdom and experience it does seem a pity not to use it all. But you know, Lord, that I want a few friends at the end.

Amen.

Beatitudes for Friends of the Aged

Blessed are they who understand
my faltering step and palsied hand.
Blessed are they who know that my ears
today
must strain to catch the things they
say.
Blessed are they who seem to know
that my eyes are dim and my wits are
slow.
Blessed are they who looked away
when coffee spilled at table today.
Blessed are they with cheery smile
who stop to chat for a little while.
Blessed are they who never say,
"You've told that story twice
today."
Blessed are they who know the ways
to bring back memories of yesterdays.
Blessed are they who make it known
that I'm loved, respected, and not
alone.

Blessed are they who know I'm at a loss
   to find the strength to carry the Cross.
Blessed are they who ease the days
   on my journey Home in loving ways.